The World Is One Place

Native American Poets Visit the Middle East

The World Is One Place

Native American Poets Visit the Middle East

edited by Diane Glancy
and Linda Rodriguez

BkMk Press
University of Missouri-Kansas City

BkMk Press
University of Missouri-Kansas City
5101 Rockhill Road
Kansas City, MO 64110
www.umkc.edu/bkmk

National
Endowment
for the Arts
arts.gov

ART WORKS.

This project is supported in part by
by the National Endowment for the Arts.

Executive Editor: Robert Stewart
Managing Editor: Ben Furnish
Assistant Managing Editor: Cynthia Beard

Cover art, "Dushara's Chair," by Kim Shuck,
photograph ©2016 by Douglas A. Salin, www.dougsalin.com

BkMk Press wishes to thank McKensie Callahan and Dana
Sanginari. Special thanks to Anders Carlson.

The views expressed by each writer in this book are his or hers alone
and do not reflect the views of the other writers, their tribes or Native
nations, or the publisher and its affiliates.

Library of Congress Cataloging-in-Publication Data

Names: Glancy, Diane, editor. | Rodriguez, Linda, editor.
Title: The world is one place : Native American poets visit the Middle East /
  edited by Diane Glancy and Linda Rodriguez.
Description: Kansas City, MO : BkMk Press, 2016.
Identifiers: LCCN 2016029741 | ISBN 9781943491070 (alk. paper)
Subjects: LCSH: American poetry--Indian authors. | Indians of North
  America--Poetry. | Middle East--Poetry.
Classification: LCC PS591.I55 W67 2016 | DDC 811/.6080897--dc23 LC
record available at https://lccn.loc.gov/2016029741

ISBN 978-1-943491-07-0

Contents

PLACE

PEOPLE

SPIRIT

Preface

Some time ago, Diane Glancy showed me a memorable cycle of poems she had written about her travels to Syria and Jordan. Later, Linda Rodriguez told me about the criticism Joy Harjo encountered after visiting Israel and, upon reflection, how many Native American writers she knew who had visited the Middle East. I then happened to mention Diane's powerful Middle East poems to her. She had the idea, and I instantly read her mind: An anthology such as this one could explore how the Middle East has captured the imaginations of such a significant group of Native American poets. What qualities of the region drew them there? What did they see? How did their cultural perspectives as Native Americans inform their reactions and insights? Both groups today live amid the aftermath of Western European expansion. Also, Native Americans serve in the US armed forces, and receive decorations and casualties, at the highest per capita rate of any ethnic group, and many have served in the Middle East. One thing led to another, and BkMk Press invited Diane to edit an anthology around several of her poems on this topic. She invited Linda to co-edit.

Ezra Pound's famous definition of literature—news that stays news—might serve as a definition of the Middle East also, since the region's sheer longevity of relevance has been more consistent than its geographic boundaries. But in assembling this anthology, the editors defined the Middle East broadly to include the Arab world, Israel, Turkey, Iran, even as far east as Afghanistan, as far west as Morocco. A couple of our contributors have visited the region only through the imagination, but almost all have made physical journeys there, many under circumstances that Diane discusses in her foreword. One contributor is an indigenous Pacific Islander, while the rest identify as Native American through tribal citizenship or through cultural participation and community recognition. This book does not purport to include all Native American poets who have been to and written about the Middle East. Some poets we approached did not have material at hand to submit, and to anyone we might have missed, our apologies.

Many Americans forget or profess not to know that Native Americans continue to exist, individually and as nations. Yet as the poets in this volume show, Native American cultures still hold a place in, and contribute to, the world community of nations, among whom they command attention and respect. Likewise, many American readers know the Middle East only through journalistic reportage of its catastrophes and conflicts. The news beat of the poet can diverge from that of the journalist, however, and while political, military, and religious unrest are inevitably part of the environments these poems depict, the poems also depart these well-documented subjects to look at the symbolic riches of even seemingly ordinary moments.

In short, I believe the world needs these poems. The views expressed by each writer in this book are his or hers alone and do not reflect the views of the other writers, their tribes or Native nations, or the publisher and its affiliates. But part of poetry's power is its ability to look squarely at the major conflicts that divide people and then to look right through them to the universal qualities that bond us all as human beings. The poets here write with distinctly knowing love and grief about what might be the world's most urgently important region today.

Ben Furnish, Managing Editor
BkMk Press, University of Missouri-Kansas City

Foreword

DIANE GLANCY, EDITOR

Syria

The earth is language.

The land essentially is story.

In March, 1994, I went to Syria and Jordan for the United States Information Agency when it was still in operation. Several years later, I traveled in Turkey on Jerome and General Mills Foundation grants.

Syria, as it turns out, would stay with me as its civil war unfolded in 2011. There were similarities to native history. The takeover of one by another. The loss of place and way of life.

I have collected notices. One from *The Independent*, published in London, May 13, 2009, "Girls Targeted in Taliban Gas Attack." The article also referred to an event, November 2008, when "men on motorbikes used water pistols to squirt acid in girls' faces as they walked to school on the outskirts of Kandahar."

I would dedicate this to the girls who want to learn.

There were connections felt in strange ways. As LeAnne Howe says in "Joy Ride, Midnight of the Cooling Winds, Amman 2010," "Shops are attached to the houses and remind me of the street in West Ada, Oklahoma." In Jordan, I thought of Utah.

It seems the land is connected, one place to another, especially having been there, one carries it thereafter. In the beehive-shaped houses in Turkey, I remembered the small mud mounds we patted together after running the hose over the backyard dirt in Kansas City.

Other Native writers made similar trips to the Middle East. This anthology is a collection of our words.

Writing, in part, is about trying to piece together experience.

And what could poetry have to do with any of it?—with its sound and imagery—its work of joining the unlikely. Its doors that open to the world that poetry makes sense of when the world does not offer explanation. An anthology, after all, is like a satellite map, each poem zeros in on one particular section of the overall story, enlarging the details thereof.

I recently made connection here in my own city, returning to the stockyards where my father came as a young man in 1928. The meat-packing houses are gone now. Armour's was razed in 1965. But the past of the stockyards is still at the confluence of the Kansas and Missouri Rivers. It took four trips to locate the ground of the old plant amid vacant lots, large storage buildings, and rows of trucks for a transport company.

Kara Evans in the Missouri Valley Special Collections at the Kansas City Public Library sent a map of the old stockyards. I eventually found the wedge of Ewing Street and State Line that opened onto Central Avenue across from which was a one-block street called, Joy. It had been the main entry to Armour's. I recalled the four- and five-story brick buildings surrounded by brick streets, over which the chute rose from the grid of cattle pens to the death-squad at the entry of the killing floor.

It is a ridiculous comparison. The trail of refugees from Syria to Jordan, Lebanon, Turkey, and Afghanistan as the great cattle trails. The cries of a wounded people in Syria, and other people in the Middle East, as it is turned into a slaughter house, is not hard to connect, though the people, even robbed of their humanity as they are, cannot be compared to cattle. I am sorry. I am sorry. But the work of finding the stockyards was more poignant as Syria itself was being razed. Finding the stockyards and piecing together an anthology of poetry about the Middle East had its similarities. All the Middle East, to some extent, is suffering annihilation by ISIS.

As of November 2016, 270,000–470,000 Syrians have died. Half of the twenty-two million population has been displaced. Eighty-three percent of the lights have gone out.

The main entry to Armour's, as I noted, was Joy Street. What an odd name for a street in the brutal stockyards. Georgia Murphy, Kansas Collection Librarian at the Kansas City, Kansas, Public Library, contacted Don Jones, who researches Kansas City, Kansas, streets. He told me the street was named after James F. Joy, an executive with the Hannibal and St. Joseph Railroad who chose Kansas City for the location of the first railroad bridge over the Missouri River. Mr. Joy may have owned some of the property where Armour Meat Packing Plant was built.

The brick buildings in the stockyards were dark brown—almost maroon. The buildings in the Middle East, on the other hand, are a light-colored mortar. The sameness was in the blasting sun that was a constant in the desert when I was there in 1994, and in the summer days of 1960 when I worked in the order supply department at Armour's after my first year at the University of Missouri.

In poetry, I can occupy two places at once. In fact, more than two. The language of place is what writing is about. It is a *re-storiation* solid as the ground that language makes.

This book is about the journeys we made to the Middle East. The words we found there. They are in the noise of a plane as it flies over the ocean from one land to another. They are on the earth below.

If poetry can be seen as the postcard of creative writing, then these poems are those cards sent from the Middle East.

The Whole of What Story

DIANE GLANCY

For a moment there was air to talk of issues—to share the
human fabric—in that brief space the U.S. spent its money
to send writers to different countries—who talked of
America—who said what it was before the military sent
the whole of the story and how the softer words are
shoveled under—and what missiles of language follow.

PLACE

Joy Harjo

I was invited to Tel Aviv in December 2012. It was a return trip to Israel, sponsored by an endowment established for women writers at the University of Tel Aviv. It wasn't my first trip to the Middle East. I have been many times, including twice to Egypt. I return to these lands whenever possible, and often in my dreams. I went as a poet, truth teller, and singer to serve justice and compassion.

My visit became intensely political because of a national campaign to force me to sign a cultural boycott. I was warned that if I didn't sign I would pay a huge price. The organization would go after me, and my reputation would be destroyed. Colleagues and friends across the country were contacted individually and urged to turn against me for not signing, to force me to sign. I felt tremendous pressure by the left. Because of threatening language, I feared for my life.

Of course I am familiar with the acts of the Israeli government and the struggle of the Palestinian people for sovereignty, for home. I'd witnessed it firsthand. During one of my first visits to Israel I saw the earliest settlements of Jewish homesteaders placed on Palestinian lands and was reminded of the injustices against my own Mvskoke Creek people. I paid close attention to the powerful eloquence of Mahmoud Darwish, one of this world's greatest poets, and the other poets I met during my journeys to the Middle East who were both Palestinian and Jewish.

I do not believe in coercing or silencing artists to serve a political end. Creative work carries the spirit of a people. Art and discourse cross political boundaries. Political boundaries in this world are established by power mongers; they are essentially lines set by war.

The campaign tactics reminded of the fervor of Christian evangelicals who recruited me to their church with candy when I was in kindergarten, where we were threatened with a demon devil to behave, and warned that their church doctrine was the only path to salvation and everyone else would go to hell if they did not believe. I left the church when I was thirteen.

I believe we exist in a universe of many kinds of trees, animals, birds, humans—we contain myriads of paths to peace and justice.

I went silent in the attack. It is obvious where I stand. I did not want to use my experiences during my visit as a form of defense. I know what love looks like, sounds like, even if it emerges through the cracks of war.

Refugee

JOY HARJO

When I was a child, I knew Bethlehem as the city of the baby Jesus.
Jesus was born in a manger, beneath a star whose rays
Bent down to give him gifts.
We give you wisdom, fortitude, and the ability to make medicine
With your words, the stars chanted.
We are all sons and daughters of God.
Cattle, sheep, and refugee parents surrounded the baby.
His parents had fled to escape a death decree against firstborn sons.
Jesus was born right there in Bethlehem, says the story.
Even the stars, they say, bended their knees.
Jesus became a healer. Walked far to help others, and to show
That we, too, are healers.
His only practice was compassion.
When he was killed by crucifixion his spirit continued walking
To remind us, we are not bound by the evil in humans.

I arrived in Bethlehem at night, with two Palestinian students
Who lived in the refugee camp in town.
Christmas light stars crisscrossed the road.
The holiday tree towered over Manger Square, waiting for
    ceremonial decoration.
We parked and went in for a snack in a local fast-food joint.
We're brothers, cousins, they said. But our status is different.
One status card was blue; one was green. One gave freedom to go
    in and out.
One locked the door and built a wall of hate and shame.
We walked across to the church built over the place where Jesus
    was born.
I felt the hope of millions shimmering there in the middle of this
    country

Torn by war. I touched the place where the manger is said to
      have stood.
I prayed for peace, that the road be blessed for these young men
      who made good
Jokes, studied hard, and liked girls.

That night they offered me a place of refuge in a home that could
      have been
My grandparents' house, or any house on tribal lands in my far-
      away country.
It was the same humble table around which we gathered, spoke,
      and ate.
I lay down to sleep in the children's room, where their sister was
      dreaming.
I listened to the human sounds of people talking their story talk,
      babies crying—
The noisy hush of a city beloved for peace all over the world.

The dark winter sky touched the shoulder of Bethlehem.
What evil has sprung up in Jesus's name—
What tight-lipped churches—
What hierarchies of rules and regulations—
What refuge.

Jim Barnes

Things and thoughts come and go. If you are lucky, sometimes an image may sneak up on you and sink a claw into your thigh. Since I am used to cats, I seldom pay much attention; but once in a while a patch of skin will tingle, and some attention must be given to the moment. Thus it was with the writing of "At Jerwan." On reading an email from Ben Furnish asking for a contribution to this anthology, I saw several images slip in through the rain that had inundated Oklahoma for most of the day—namely, images returning from the faraway and foggy days of graduate school when I thought it necessary to saturate myself in the Romantics. Images from Sennacherib's terrible rush for glory and Ozymandias's crumbling legacy in particular seemed to want to stay. What Byron and Shelley perceived important two hundred years ago is just as relevant today. Their view for the end of lust for power was dust and destruction, all that may be left of the Middle East in our own time. But who can say where poems truly come from or what their cause? "At Jerwan" scratched, and I let it in. Though I have spent but little time in the Middle East—Turkey—but many years among heavy tomes, perhaps I should quote Keats's memorable line about traveling in the realms of gold.

At Jerwan

JIM BARNES

Stretching to the south toward Nineveh
the fertile lands Sennacherib
surveyed have now neither grain nor gold
for the hand holding compass and fold.

Long before the droning night came
down for the spoils and the wind with blame
for the deadly absence and the fall,
frowning figures left their places

on crumbling marble monuments
and sank into the dry river bed
where the hot hand that fell still means
to fall on the holy heads of gods.

No gardens hanging from the banks,
no stone aqueducts now standing
lone, level, or otherwise.

        Far from
Ishtar and Nineveh only this:
dust, thirst, desert despair,
the dream of Sennacherib gone wrong.

PLACE

Goshen Tavern

JIM BARNES

And I will sustain you there . . . .
—Genesis 45:11

Homing in
through pitch dark
fog and firs,
you find the tavern
announced by
blue neon.

Inside:
your eyes ache
from the road.

you drink from
a bottle marked
with mountains.

This is Oregon,
you say, and the land
is plenty hard
to know.

There
is no one to hear,
but you, exile,
say it anyway.

Bojan Louis

1.

My initial goal was to write about the alternative metal band System of a Down, the members of which hail from Armenia, it being their birthplace or their parents' birthplace, or by way of Lebanon. In 2006, the documentary *Screamers*, which examined why genocide happens, and has happened, in contemporary society, was released and featured System of a Down. It focused on their activism concerning "modern day" genocide(s), specifically with the Armenian genocide (from which their grandparents and parents suffered) and Turkey's refusal to acknowledge its occurrence, as well as, the United States' apathetic stance, since it likes to utilize a Turkish airbase. According to activist, journalist, and professor Samantha Power, a screamer is one who voices that an atrocity is happening, that a people are being annihilated. Voices—not allowed (accepted) to be heard. Silenced, perhaps? All the same, they scream to call attention.

2.

Turkey and the city of Istanbul have fascinated me since youth. To me they are places steeped in myth, dense, and yet familiar; lamb is cuisine. The more I learned about Turkey and the more I believed I understood, ultimately I became more unable to write about the country and city. How could I place values on an area and people that I didn't belong to?

3.

Some months after visiting Istanbul and the Cappadocia region of Turkey (or was it some months before?), I met a young Armenian woman in a Philly dive who happened to know, actually know, the members of System of a Down. She was originally from Los Angeles, where SOAD was formed. We chatted a few times over spliffs, cigarettes, and lagers; she'd tell me of her uncle pointing toward Armenia, the consequences. This must have occurred before my and the woman's generation, right? In the end, we'd leave a lot unsaid about genocide. We understood, knew, it.

4.

Hitler is said to have expressed that if the United States could forget its genocide of its indigenous peoples—Turkey of the Armenians—then who would bat an eye over the Jews? There are claims and research that his concentration camps were based on his study of Bosque Redondo, the final destination of the Navajo Long Walk; genocide feasibly efficient thanks to starvation and nefarious combat tactics.

5.

It's easy to forget the larger, complete story, and accountability; convenient to know highlights, a here-and-there fact. It's impossible to go back and say, "*you* did this harm to me." Forgivable to say, "yes, it was *me*."

To Sugar a Dream

BOJAN LOUIS

I'm told, sounds close
to the original tongue.

No question, says the owner of a spot
called Jimmy's, any other Turk will *know*
you mean: *teşekkür ederim.*

I tell him *ahxéhee* as he rolls up a rug
depicting Noah's flood.

Hands it over, says, impossible for me.

Every town I visit beyond the city,
I'm tempted to ask,
What's with Armenia?

Everyone's forgotten, yeah?

Direct your arm east and encounter its breaking,
silence after the reset fracture: sedatives caress.

Recall lagers in a Philly dive around 4AM
where a woman relayed the above—

an uncle's twig-bent limb
cracked out a hurried cast.

Never direct your murderer's gaze back
to any origin where land drooled bone,
towns or settlements turned scab.

Instead, help snip the thread of sewn-shut lips.

And, scream inside until the hum of it weakens organs, dulls brain.

Listen to music you don't like, stare at televisions bolted to the ceiling.

Don't forget to say, thank you, always.

Kimberly Blaeser

My visit to the Kingdom of Bahrain came in the October before the Arab Spring. Many of the writers there seemed filled with an urgency, burning to share their own experiences. Some of the moving poems I was given while there I quote in my readings or use in classes, such as this short poem by Karim Radhi:

WAR MINISTER

He was appointed minister of homicide
After he failed in agriculture, education, and health.

My experiences, though, also included meetings with students, joyful meals by the sea, visits to the vibrant souk, a wonderful individualized visit to the grand mosque, and rich, leisurely conversations. Every experience had its own resonance, but one that continues to visually haunt me was driving out of the city of Manama and seeing the newly built Royal University for Women rising from the desert. As I suggest in one of my poems, it seemed like a mirage— appearing there solid and stately, as if simply conjured by desire alone. It was five years new when I visited, and the faculty felt driven to empower the young women in their charge.

I was not surprised by the activism of the writers in the uprising of the next spring and, like many, voiced support for Ayat Al-Qurmezi who was arrested for reciting a poem in Pearl Square.

The people of Bahrain generously shared their culture and their struggles. I remain inspired by my time there.

Voices in the Desert, Bahrain 2010

KIMBERLY BLAESER

Newly sprung from the windswept earth
miles from Manama's sleek seaport of spires and glass,
the *Royal University for Women*—business, IT, art and design,
seeking *voice in decision making*, a *gender-just society*
rising here like a mirage within the ancient world.

> *After birth*
> *the woman is given*
> *a ritual cup*
> *and three dried figs.**

Under these sand-colored walls of change
smiling together the veiled and unveiled—
no custom older than education,
none more predictable than the portico picture.

> *The baby's umbilical cord is buried*
> *in the mosque if it is a boy*
> *in the kitchen if it is a girl.*

Runway fabrics glitter and sway desire, flash color;
workshop students study the drape of tradition
redrawing fashion lines, show ankle and arm—
the cant of fashion, too, as universal as story
as gendered as ritual.

> *A rooster or a chicken is slaughtered.*

*Text in right column taken from an exhibit at Bahrain National Museum in Manama.

PLACE

Shiteet, the Smallest Pearl

KIMBERLY BLAESER

When color and scale of languages
give way to simple b & w of gesture,

When clocks mark prayer five times
each day & chanting voices call,

When your expert hands smooth
wrap & arrange the *hijab* on my head,

Now silently within the Al-Fateh Mosque
belief kneels beside belief.

Fatima at the Bab el-Bahrain Souk

KIMBERLY BLAESER

Brandishing tales of gender-separate wedding parties
and Hollywood-esque female glamour,
you slide your delicate wrist into blue evil-eye bracelets
spread before me the protective *hamsa*.
When obedience is the old wealth, freedom the new,
how to find hands to hold in the fray—
a talisman or safety that cuts both ways?
We finger gold cartouche, amulets, sacred cloth,
even clipped verses from the Quran
deflectors that wake doubt in our own brown eyes:
A protection from every rebellious devil!

PLACE

Unlawful Assembly

KIMBERLY BLAESER

Don't hurry to safety.
Each hour your flowered room grows smaller.
Everywhere at the periphery of vision
windows shatter into triangles
of mosaic light.
There in the lonely fragments
a youtube dictator
declares victory,
blood flattens and darkens.
The scent of rebellion
smoke fire and ash
all pungent in the still images
sacrificed to history.
Somewhere the flapping door of an overturned wagon
thumps steadily
in a deserted street—
echoes absent hands.

Before Pearl Square

KIMBERLY BLAESER

Official awards are given, winners feted. Now one hour grows
into three and still all eyes follow dark language. My books piled
to one side, your poems spread before me like the memory of
treaty documents. Translation changes *government* to a word more
nearly meaning *victor*.
That I understand, won't change the jobless poor.
That you tell—is another word for *danger*.

Diane Glancy

My focus is the civil war in Syria. In some way, it tells me about the Native past. The removal trail, the injustice, the massacres. It holds truth to the past. It shares a post with Native history. If there had been video cameras and embedded reporters in the Indian wars of the 19th century, there would be a visual archive of the Trail of Tears, the atrocities at Wounded Knee, the Black Kettle Grasslands, Sand Creek, and all the lesser-known massacres such as the Marias Massacre in Montana when the 2nd Cavalry attacked a Piegan camp, January 23, 1870.

An independent film by Talal Derki, *Return to Homs,* aired on POV, PBS, July 20, 2015, as a look behind the barricades of the besieged Syrian city of Homs, "where, for 19-year-old, Abdul Basset al-Saroot and his ragtag group of comrades, the audacious hope of revolution is crumbling like buildings around him."

The rebels and the Free Syrian Army declared a refusal to bow on March 18, 2011. The atrocities in Syria followed.

News coverage of the uprisings was not permitted, so the small protest group was filmed covertly. Saroot narrates the film. He sings protest songs to inspire and incite the people to resist the Syrian regime of Bashar al-Assad. "We want to live with freedom and dignity. The age of oppression will end. To become a martyr has been my dream for years. My other dream is victory. With my blood, father, we shall please God. Our land bleeds. The land is sad. The children cry, but who is listening?"

The regime begins firing tear gas. It posts barricades prohibiting the movement of traffic. It begins torture, murder, and the mortar shelling of buildings until they look like sweaters filled with moth-holes. "Bashar al-Assad kills his own people to keep his seat."

The regime stopped bombing when the UN made their hour-and-a-half inspection of the torn city. Saroot says the rebels lost the big war after being confident over the smaller victories. There are scenes of the wounded rebels. "Could we use a magnet to pull out the shrapnel?" someone asks in a makeshift hospital. "No, shrapnel is aluminum." "O Lord may you accept him," a man cries as his comrade dies.

"What are you waiting for?" Saroot asks the West. "But the world remains silent as a graveyard. Where's the road out? I am going to the land of the lions. The dream dies. Homs is destroyed. God is all we have left."

The independent film does not address ISIS, which formed after US withdrawal from Iraq and Afghanistan, and was well on its way during the filming. The Syrian rebels now have ISIS as well as the regime to resist. On August 18, 2015, Khaled al-Assad, an 83-year-old antiquities scholar and government director of Syria's ancient ruins of Palmyra was beheaded in the main square. Afterward, they hung his body on a pole. The extremists believe ancient relics promote idolatry. ISIS saw Khaled al-Assad as the director of idols. I would dedicate my part of this anthology to the Syrian rebels who refuse to bow. I also dedicate it to history, to ancient ruins, and to those who uphold them in the war against artifact and culture that preserve whatever remains of humanity are left in the latest barbarous and accelerated wave of injustice.

Down to the Simplest Wire in the Human Voice

DIANE GLANCY

1.

Once I was in a van in Syria. The roads were like riding
a camel. There was desert cluttered with pebbles that
seemed rubble, but was standard for the houses in
villages made of stone and mortar

and next door the olive orchards and women picking
there. Or doing the work in fields where the country
was broken into with mountains and of course
the Mediterranean Sea.

By day, I traveled place to place, making steady passage
into the distance. I took notes on the passing land—a
bump in the road, and the words I wrote could not be
read. Or I made run-on statements of what I saw. *There is
brightness of sunlight there is remoteness*—until I
looked for meaning in my notes and found none though
I looked under the mountains and in the sea.

At night, the open windows. The dark sea by Jableh.
The waves of Arabic language rich with a new horizon.
I saw the eyes of people floating with curiosity
and mine at them as well.

2.

Every time I left a town I took the view of a boat
leaving the sea vacant there on the shore
as if the whole world were a broken slice of the moon
across the Mediterranean.

I tell you these valleys will run with blood
if these wars of nations continue—
these open, running sores
in the general way the world is moving
as if draining to a close

the way I shut my purse with a click
in the Damascus marketplace, the *suk*,
the burro with his dosser, the stalls of meat, the home-
spun silver pin I bought.

3.
Yet the road rippled as though a field
where an ancient farmer plowed his furrows,
and from my viewpoint,
when I saw more soldiers with their guns,
I knew no one in my country could tell me what
to believe
and I was happy about it.

Those beliefs have to come from within
or I would be at odds
as I was the day I went to the Muslim school for girls
and my heart sat a little at their desks, and the door
for me was in the leaving which they could not,
and among them were the people I met and spoke at.
They were kind you see and allowed me to talk
as the sun scrubbed the lovely sea at their port city
on the coast at Lattakia.

Wherever I went
the loudspeaker from a minaret read from the Koran
of the Islam religion into the streets.
What if they piped the Bible into my own country on the
corner of Market and Elm?

As I passed through Aleppo and Homs on my way back
to Damascus I thought of the bylaws of my own
country—
the triune system of Capitalism for greed,
Democracy for altruism,
the Judeo-Christian heritage for a moral component.
And the Syrian road where the apostle Paul was
dumbstruck two thousand years ago
was brought right up front at last.

Something far away and remote
weighted its place in my bones.
Discontinuities or something like that
because of the conflicts and contradictions
in the human heart.

Histrionics

DIANE GLANCY

1.

In the night, in the strange bed in a foreign land, I had a
vision of a night sky with stars. The stars were yellow
and they flicked like fireflies over a swamp in high
summer.

I saw a black sky filled with stars. As if a dress sewn
with electric elk teeth. They had a buzz of their own.
Yellow *starz* they could be called.

I thought it was time to go to the afterlife. I waited.
Maybe an elk would come to show me where to step off
the earth into the sky I saw. My heart rumbled in my
chest.

My rhumba heart.

I thought the sky would come down over me like a teepee,
the lining of which would be zipped with stars.
Everything's gone modern. Even the stars move to some
new source. *That's where we go, the ancestors say.* You
know if you've ever had a front row seat somewhere, what
it's like when you can see everything close up. That's
where I thought I was. But I'd just woke from sleeping
through a night. After about five hours anyway. Because
I was in a time zone still off. But there was nowhere I
could go without the guide, the driver, the embassy van. I
thought I should just stay in bed, caught in a place I could
not leave. But I had a companion that was the night sky
filled with those yellow *starz*. Space is not space, but
cluttered with bodies floating here and there as if your

room was full of flyers and you had to duck or you'd hit
your head on them.

2.

I thought of who I would see. Jesus, of course, and the
Bible people I've wanted to see. They'd be off there in
their desert tents in space, but I could stop. It was like
sitting on Mount Nebo in Jordan and looking across the
Dead Sea into Israel. *Something like Utah*, the woman
said who drove me there. It wasn't a tour bus but a private
trip. Like this one out to the stars. Close up, there are
many more than we can see. Even more we can't see
sparking like buffalo. But I wasn't a Plains Indian as they
expected. I was from a woodland tribe originally from
the Southeast. The point from where the Cherokee people
walked to Oklahoma before it was even that. Maybe the
sky I saw was an early settlement. What the heavens
looked like before it got to be heaven. When all the stars
roamed like a herd we know was once on this continent.

And who else would I see? My father, of course, with
his black eyes and hair. My mother. The relatives I
knew. Mostly I want to see those I didn't know. My
father's people who were gone before I got here. I tried to
remember if I'd seen them on my way. I was coming
about the time they left. Maybe we passed. You know
those memories you don't know where they come from.
The way you know a black sky filled with yellow elk
teeth can move your dress even after you sew them on,
and you wake in the morning and see the fleck-light you

 PLACE

received in the darkness of this earth away from what
matters to your heart, and you say *holy God* because you
learned to pray according to the churches of your world.
It's where your home is, your father told you, and lived
away from it all his life, though he knew the sky was
waiting. I remember when I knew he was leaving. Not
that afternoon. No, it was several years later. But the
vision of his death appeared.

3.
So now for a companion I have a night sky filled with
stars. As if there was a sale on them. As if I was in
surplus city where they'd been shelved from all the nights
instead of in a foreign land—the militant buzz—the
undercurrent of Allah—Allah—the power of something
not mine—against mine.

Star City—I think of the avenue through which I'd walk
to Christ the Christian religion taught. That we married
God. No. We married Christ. He was the groom who
waited for us at the end of life. Or who was coming again
through the stars. Or sky. As if I was early at a wedding
and had to sit there alone until the others arrived.

The stars were fireflies that attended. Or insects carrying
candles or those pencil flashlights.

4.
You know each attempt to talk stubs the dark. But you
open your mouth. The words will light their fingers as
you talk.

You want to say about visions, they're true but maybe in a time to come. Or they're saying something now but you can't figure it out. Or in a certain combination of circumstances you'll know. Even though you feel you should be doing something in response to your vision if only you understood the sky at night. There were stars as if the sun had burst and filled the vast air of space with particles. They were thick as leaves you didn't want to rake, and have them all there facing you one afternoon when you decide you'd better rake your yard before it rains or snows and they pack like a concrete slab.

You try to remember if you'd seen that vision of stars before. You know when you were little and saw things on the ceiling of your room.

5.
While I listened for stories I did not hear my ears had fallen like dried mud puddles around my knees.

It's why I lift my knee to your mouth to hear your words. Tell me why the sky is black and pocked with yellow.

Tell me, Father, about Abraham in the desert hearing his children would be like the stars.

Necessary Departures

DIANE GLANCY

You clunk your boot in the updust of religion.
There is no lightness here.

The forces rally in their own divided land.
It's hard to straddle the old argument:

Cain with the crops of his field,
Abel with the lamb

as he must have been instructed.
What floats inland as the only boat,

militant, avenging.
You see them in the shadows,

you hear them on the screen
grounding a different ground

than yours to stand on,
your indivisibility divided into units.

Not the justice you knew
when you heard the verdict

as we move toward the holy wars
at the headwaters of the world.

PLACE

PEOPLE

Linda Hogan

We were in this town. There was an old stone church. These dancers came out and danced for us. They put us in a kind of trance. I wanted to stay there forever. This poem was my way to capture and preserve that extraordinary experience.

The Night in Turkey

LINDA HOGAN

I forget too many things
but I will never forget the dancers
in the stone church out far in the country.
It was night. The milk in the cold sky
was strongly drawn.
Inside we sat with tea
and the men came out,
nodded at one another, just men
in white robes
and it seems music began
but that I can barely remember
because the men began encircling themselves
at the very core of life
and whirling, stepped in together,
their robes opening out
like tender flowers in first spring.

It seemed the sky unfurled
in all its starlit splendor,
one white moon in the darkness
after another
and the world began to bloom warm again.
The human all had vanished
as we were entranced
and nothing in this world could have missed it.

All this, all this, because something in the human
was silenced and dancers opened in their life
to something greater in the darkness
and we were there with them,
as we became one of them
in a world that bloomed one winter night
from inside a dark building of stone
that fell away from all of us.

Kim Shuck

At university I became curious about ancient cultures on the east coast of the Mediterranean, in the Fertile Crescent. I think that it started with tablet weaving and moved on to Jerusalem, and at that point there were any number of interesting technologies and poetries to explore. Petra became one of my must-see places. The opportunity came up to go to a poetry conference in Jordan that would tour Petra, and I couldn't say yes fast enough.

Jordan exceeded my expectations. Everywhere we went, if people were told that we were poets, they would sit down and wait for a poem. English-speaking or not, people wanted to hear them. I felt very well taken care of by Jordanians, particularly the Bedouin people I met there. Among the other great gifts I had from Jordan was a brother who is also a poet. I loved the heat and the food and the tempo of life. I loved the decorated trucks we saw on every street. I loved hearing the calls to prayer through the day. I loved Petra. Petra is breathtaking. There are carvings here and there that surprised me. The camel on the road down into the city was particularly wonderful. Every poem I wrote there was a love letter to the people. Politics, stereotypes in all directions, whatever other thing might stand between us, I enjoyed my visit, the people that I met there, and, given a good opportunity, I'd go back without thinking twice.

In the Southern Desert

KIM SHUCK

The white camel is pregnant we
Drink sage tea with cinnamon eat
Popcorn and listen to her sing to the
Sandstone sing to the
Cisterns that we are later shown with
Nabatean petroglyphs in an
Almost invisible fold of rock we eat
Popcorn and lean on saddles we
Listen to the pregnant white camel and stories of
T.E. Lawrence the pink sand gets everywhere
Saleh says it's like sugar and that
Sugar is life the sparrows have
Pink bellies
Desert pink and the swallows kite there are
Feet carved into the rock near the
Water there are
Feet there and the water works its way through
Sandstone and here in the dry I can smell the
Sweet water

Down the Siq

KIM SHUCK

Dushara does not sit in the chair they carved for him and some of the
Stones breathe in the wind they
Breathe like the absent god
Does it matter who is
Witness?
Orange kittens they tell me the kittens are wild
Roll and
Wrestle through tourist goods at the
Top of the Siq we sit and have more tea
Black with cardamom and cinnamon in the
Dark the heat drains and the kittens play with my
Bootlaces shocking blue
Lizards scratch and rummage out of reach
Dushara is not in his chair on the cliff face but
We can hear the stones breathing with the
Catch and tempo of old things the
Tea is good and I pull a bag of almonds from my bag
Offer them as part of our feast
Everyone takes at least one and a sleepy kitten curls against my
Foot we each
Take a cup of tea down the Roman road to the
Treasury to the tombs lit with candles there is
Music and more chairs for the
Invisible god he must be
Busy does it matter how we
Witness? An olive tree
Shows where the water is there in the
Marketplace the guards sometimes sleep in the old
Well the old well is
Cool

Water to Water

KIM SHUCK

I've splashed my feet in the
Jordan River and been answered by a
Fish who also splashed they are
Digging there up the road digging
Ancient things buildings this time we are
Taken from water to water this river the
Dead Sea the
Hospitality of tea we are taken to the old
Ruins and fresh mint tea I stare at the
Embroidery for too long shapes familiar
Shapes my fingers have made fall in love with
Rosewater and honey we are
Slow together we remember things but it's
All tied together with knots of water with
Heart water

James Thomas Stevens

I have not written of my time in Jordan until now, though it is vivid in my mind. Invited to an ill-fated international poetry festival, Natives all, we had been chosen to represent the United States. When the invite came, we began calling one another asking, "Is this real? The airline tickets, the itineraries, the resort hotels?" One by one, we began to receive our tickets and things became very real.

On the flight over, a grandmother traveling with her young granddaughters had a medical emergency and passed away, forcing us to land in Roma for a few hours —this was an omen of things to come. As we arrived on our different flights, we were informed that, due to one of the American organizers giving an Israeli poet an "Indian name" and trying to dupe the Jordanian writers, funding had been pulled. We were taken, not to the scheduled resort, but to a small hotel on the dusty outskirts of Amman. Some of the group simply holed up in their rooms and bided their time in Jordan.

My recollections are of four of us who decided to take advantage of this opportunity to meet the local people of Amman, to take buses and taxis to the Dead Sea, Petra, and Jerash. We befriended college students, cab drivers, and even a young, hip Bedouin at Petra. One photo from the trip inspired the poem, "We Are." In it, fellow poets, Jennifer Fox Bennett (Anishinaabe), Jeremy Arviso (Diné, Hopi, Pima, Tohono O'odam) and I stand atop steps at the Dead Sea with our arms raised in the air. We were four experiencing the generosity and friendliness of our Jordanian hosts, their willingness to share food, laughter, and poetry.

We Are

JAMES THOMAS STEVENS

We were four
at the market place in
Amman's al-Balad. Lakota,
Anishinaabe, Pueblo, and Mohawk.

Cubist hills rolling
out from us. Concrete cliffs
    to cloudless sky.

They were two
asking, *Where from? Who?*
Yes. America, but no.
The only way to signify—a feather
at the back of the head.

Sauvagi!
We register
displeasure—*a yes, but no.*

A third offers, *Al honood al humr.* Explains, *Red Indians.*

Four
in the rust blue city of Petra, before
the gaping façade of al-Khazneh.
Knit-capped children playing with puppies
in sandstone homes.

She was one,
urban rebel in jeans and
army boots, a black hijab
    around her face.

Excited to show off Amman,
she packed us into a cab, headed toward
the university district.

We were five, sitting in The Doors Café,
Jim Morrison endless, over
the effervescence
    of bubbling nargilehs.

A dark back room in a blinding white city.

We were many
at the tomb of King Hussein. Lakota,
Anishinaabe, Pueblo, Cheyenne, Tsalagi
    and Mohawk.

There for a poetry festival
that would never occur, instead we honored
a dead king with a tobacco ceremony, read
poems in people's homes, in deserts, in cafés.

They were many
that offered so readily, on buses,
in sweet shops, in taxi cabs . . .

You have no family here, so we are your family.
Here, take this bag of dates for your trip.
I am a nurse. Take my card in case any of you have need.
Come, eat with my family and we will share words.

Travis Hedge Coke

I was asked to come to Jordan as part of a festival to promote international peace and unity. It was a flawed operation and our primary objective became, in honesty, a variation on *first do no harm*. Nonetheless, it was an amazing experience, and I hope we did some good for more than only ourselves. Jordan was, and is, a wonderful country, on whose soil and floors I felt more secure than I often have in my home country. It was my first journey to the other side of the planet, and I was both overwhelmed and incredibly honored by that.

My interaction with, and attention to the region did not end with that trip, of course, though I have not physically returned there. I have friends and colleagues who are there, time to time. The news and both political and social actions there affect us all. Israel, specifically colonization and border aggression, was the topic of the first serious, *careful* conversation a girlfriend and I ever had. These things affected how I wrote and how I write now regarding a region of understated influence and, quite often, very good poetry.

Some Old Adage

TRAVIS HEDGE COKE

I can't believe
beside the door
my mom, I think it's my mom
this land
this lamp
my lamb, I think it's my lamb
dead at the time, but it's still a war
one light, one glass bulb and shade shaped like a flower that does
    not light
sorry works when you stop shooting

no one sees a horse when it's a mile behind them
no one sees a cat the color of sand out there
not with each other we're going to fight
pressed foil in Irbid, minutes from Pella
stone lasts at least as long as rubies or the dogs
paisley women with cool eyes judging the rolled bones

blue faceted rubies
I may have been staring at them too long
in old sunlight
under lamplight
if the lamp would light like its twin its cousin its
cousin
I think it's my cousin
my land

Rifke

TRAVIS HEDGE COKE

Rifke is a step ahead of buddha
Rifke is a stride before thunder
Rifke is the blue yawn of distant sky
Rifke in the kitchen hanging chilis
bringing up the bright dawn

The curtains got mud
the birds all carry falcon's shields
in this weird rhythm
far from when they killed most of us

boom boom I don't remember that anyway
she says under the gun

"Get outta my face"
Rifke does not have time for you
"you ain't that pretty
and your impatience annoys me"

shoo shoo I'm not interested anyhow
before you've even begun

In the old desert
and in the new-built city block
Rifke in a new
dress the length of shadows and love

sure sure you are, hon
she says in the sun

Slow smile better than yours, Rifke gives it
Rifke's talk is fast, like a brave cornet
She has a movement beyond even you
Rifke stands with her shoulder to the brick
and her face in the sun

Standing in a Garden Rose

TRAVIS HEDGE COKE

disappear
while I, not dead, watch cold, white sun descend behind
whips of delicate eighty-five dollar coffee
disappear in the rain, from sight of
of bread, laughing cloud and warm
mountain made close
too get to my feet . . . stop . . . laughing . . . too under an oak . . . to be
sun over its quota of frustration.stops
    HOVERS
extra moments light
under economically incessant flocking and scene life
gunmetal current, clinging to rocks at
the base of—cling to rocks at the base of—It's been a long cliff
lose slice decline of light
    SLOW drink, enjoying flavor texture soon gone

I also partake of distressingly long time.

Touch

TRAVIS HEDGE COKE

this way
it turns like a compass
she holds the cutting edge in the water

they pass through my pillowcase
maybe it's cartilage
what holds the feathers onto them

the air won't darken
corkscrew migrations
from air to water at night

Trevino L. Brings Plenty

Research Proposal
Email sent August 27, 2005

Hello Everyone,

I arrived in Amman, Jordan. I am alive. There has been some trouble before we arrived. It was rumored that an Israeli was to read at this event. Not true. This was a Native American living in Israel.

There was slanderous press all around. Most of the festival was cancelled. I will be returning to the States earlier than I thought.

I have made great contacts here with the other writers. The Jordanians are wonderful people. As in the States, people read sound bites and take it at face value. It was a lot of propaganda by some of the Jordanian poets protesting the event. I was interviewed with local news. A lot of work is going to happen tomorrow. We, the original People of the Americas, will go to the US embassy and hold a reading. We will invite the Jordanian poets and make as much peace as possible.

(As I speak a wedding is going on outside the office. Fireworks can be heard in the distance.)

On the flight here a Palestinian died of a heart attack. We visited the Kings' Family Tomb. This is rare, even for the locals to be allowed to do.

Hopefully with the connections made I will go visit the rest of the world.

My trip is half over. Amman, Jordan, reminds me of a densely populated US reservation. I will write further of my trip when I get home.

Much Love from Amman, Jordan,
Trevino L. Brings Plenty

The Same Question Asked in Jordan

TREVINO L. BRINGS PLENTY

It wasn't until
I visited Petra
that it became clear.

A Bedouin seated on his donkey
asked where I was from.
I looked Japanese to him, but not quite.
My long black hair tied back,
brown arms and face as
dark as rich soil.

I tried to say
in poorly pronounced Arabic
that I was a Red Indian,
though this descriptor didn't fit me.
American barely fit.
Indian,
American Indian,
Native American,
never said much
of who I am.

The Bedouin
who was not
much younger than me
understood
what I was trying
to say to him and smiled.
He pointed his

brown finger at me
and said,
"You are a Bedouin."

I nodded in acceptance.
I couldn't say
much more.
I reached out
my empty hand and
shook his empty hand.

My First Pair of the Dead Sea

TREVINO L. BRINGS PLENTY

I am a 240 pound, six foot one, Lakota male with long hair.
I don't have a six pack washboard stomach. My trunk is a pony keg.

The Dead Sea heat is moving my bowels to foul.
What despair to travel desert miles
to finally reach a large body of water
and have it be salted, undrinkable.

The red clay shore caking my feet,
the unbearable blue of the Dead Sea before me.
There is only a half rack of bacteria alive in it.

The day before I walked ruin in Jerash.
Now blisters popped,
I step into the uncomfortably warm water.

My Achilles heel is safe,
but the blisters burn
with precision pin prick pangs.
The water is greasy on my skin.
I can't dip my body into this Dead Sea body.
I have to wait it out.

I stand on the shore.
I find it strange to pay
an entrance fee to this public beach.

Dead Sea swimmers rub the sea floor clay on their skin.
This clay is pH balanced. It must be a creation story
to see all these people covered with clay

for the sake of pretty skin. I rub the clay on my legs,
rinse off in the open air shower,
my legs are shiny
with the hair greasy, matted to my skin.

There are only a few Arabic women, fully clothed mostly.
There are tourists here. I am one of them.

I squat on the clay shore,
smoke a French cigarette,
spit to my side, endure the heat,
feel the salt burn my soles.

It took the Dead Sea for me to purchase,
for my large Lakota frame,
my first pair of Speedos.

With my arms crossed, muscles sore,
feet and skin on fire,
I stare at the Arabic sun.

Damn, I look Dead Sea good.

Amman

TREVINO L. BRINGS PLENTY

This desert city of song,
I stand on a hotel roof,
watch my first sunset close the Jordan day.

Across the street is a cinder block shack.
Old tires lay on its roof. It reminds me
of my grandparents' home.

My pockets are empty
except for a palm-sized hand drum.
My head is filled with melody.
I tap the drum with my index finger.
My shoes are not yet dusted clean.
My feet move in rhythm.
I will walk downtown and sing.

I can't read any of the shop signs.
I carry a blue pen with me
and pieces of blank paper.
I confess my love of a city so far away from home.

I quickly walk across a street,
the road is slick and illuminated
by headlights and mosques emptying its prayers.

In the exhaust fumes,
the air coats my lungs
and I wonder at any war for the sake of petty control.

I have nothing from the war against my blood.
I was made by genocide's wrath.
My language was prohibited,
my songs were writhing dreams
of a people who wanted life.

I am alive. I sing to myself songs older than the air I breathe.

I sing in the Amman streets.

I will always sing for home.

Monday, March 28, Private Dinner Hosted by Bohemian Syrian Writers and Dissidents

DIANE GLANCY

I met a beautiful man who'd cooked chicken and rice and there was salad and other dishes on the table of his apartment. I hugged him when I left, held my head against his chest too long. We shared a kiss delicious as the meal, and he who said no English, said, stay with me. I couldn't, of course, you know regrets the next morning, the responsibility of responsible behavior, the diligent heart of a diligent nation.

But I would like to have, and felt brittle as my papers when they dried after I left them on the porch in the morning rain. He still holds me against him as if our ancestors long ago had left one behind when the other started out to reach a new land, because they loved the sea, because they loved travel, because they loved most of all the nomad of the human heart, or the camel-train starting out now toward the stars, because we're not satisfied, but striving down the ages to hold one another in that separation, that necessary departure, we're still having to leave.

A Bedouin Girl Reads about Transportation in Russia

DIANE GLANCY

1.
March 31–April 2, Jordan

On the road, the three-wheeled trucks overloaded
with people,
the hexagonal side-panels of metal,
silver, red, green,
like strange banners in a cathedral,
an ostrich feather on the grille.

2.
Above Amman, in the mountains, remote, windy, rainy,
a barefoot girl, a Bedouin, reads a schoolbook
the interpreter says is on Russian transportation.

If you told her how reading all that
she's behind the world's traffic
as she's ever been in your western thought.
She's reading wrong and out of date. Their trucks would
be your junkyard, and you know how your country's
arrogance makes you smug and you unwrap it like a tick
as if it's simply uncontested.

The armed soldiers stand at checkpoints on the shore
where Russia peddles its hype to those who cannot know

the *jabals,*
wadis,
the windy villages, concrete-walled and cold-floored.

3.

You're a visitor to a country near the beginning of
history. You've entered the mess of influence
competing with interpretation. You fear your own heart,
and clear away with your only hand the barefoot
Bedouin girl in her village you pass through wanting to
say you're from a country of transportation, but you
know how seeing another country makes you see your own
and you know how America's eye is always on itself.

4.

And when the Arab Writers' Union asks why America
favors Israel you say your country likes Democracy,
you say you're from a Judeo-Christian heritage,
Islam was not in your Bible except what departed with
Ishmael from Isaac,
you went to school with Jews.

5.

On your return to Amman you see the iron rods
the *hadid qudban* that stick up from the corners
of cement buildings because it means
they plan to build more
and because they look like lodge poles in a teepee
having your land taken
the Palestinians relate to you and you relate to the
occupied territories you see from the other side of the
Dead Sea
like the Arabs' trucks dressed as gypsy tents with green /
red stripes and feathers for hood ornaments their glories
are in their going, their *yes* on the road galloping
between the hills as horses into a battle they think
they're destined to win.

SPIRIT

LeAnne Howe

A March rainstorm is the image I carry of my life in Jordan. I'm shopping at the corner market one block from my apartment in Amman. It's 2011 and hasn't rained for nearly a year. Then suddenly the clouds open and sheets of raindrops the size of silver dollars fall on the dusty streets. Mr. Farhan, the greengrocer, is the first to dart outside followed by his customers, their families, even a truck driver delivering oranges. Like giggling children we hold our hands up to catch the rain. Others chant *alhamdulillah* and weep openly. So do I. The downpour continues for almost an hour. Later, dripping wet, we return inside to shop for zucchini, potatoes, and onions. The cash register remains open just as Mr. Farhan left it. Jordanian dinars and coins are tossed across the top of the drawer in haste. No one cares about money when you can drink the rain.

I've lived in Jordan off and on for the past 23 years. Early in 1992 I took my first trip to Jordan and Israel, and the experience marked me in ways I'm still ferreting out, from the major floods I lived through in southern Jordan in 1993 to the ongoing drought in 2011. I was a Fulbright scholar at the University of Jordan, 2010–2011. One memory that stands out concerns a class I was teaching on American Indian literatures and climate change. I was explaining that in the 1830s, Southeastern tribes were being removed by the thousands to Indian Territory and that, they too, were experiencing climate changes. In my lecture I was soft-peddling today's climate change when a graduate student auditing the class finally raised his hand. "Professor, we know about global warming. Look around. We live in the desert and our country is full of refugees. Thousands of Syrians are crossing our borders daily to escape being killed. There is no water in Jordan. Unless we manage rainfall, we will all die." The student was from the tribe of Beni Ḥassān, one of the larger tribes in Jordan. He was well spoken and polite but very troubled. Many Beni Ḥassān clans still depend on grasslands for raising sheep. The drought had wiped out much of the open grasslands and the sheep were dying. The price of a single sheep had more than doubled in 2011.

I have hundreds of images of Jordan that I carry. Memories. I can say without hesitancy that in some ways when I return to Jordan, I always feel at home, although it isn't "home." Perhaps the reason is because Jordan is a nation of tribes and immigrants. In that respect Jordan is much like Oklahoma, my homeland.

Yes, Bilaad ash Sham

LEANNE HOWE

One thousand years before arriving in *Bilaad ash Sham*, tribesmen had whispered over the sands, always late at night, inculcating each grain with a factual detail of the narrative. Often the plot intertwined, other times the grains of sand refracted against one another to alter the telling of their magnificent conquests and illusive defeats, of how their ancient grandfathers had suffered their semen into the wombs of young women from the southern tip of Yemen to the interior of Hejaz, and of those women they had loved truly, they must now once again die for.

The Weather Five Years Ago

LEANNE HOWE

A sand storm last night, yesterday, from the Arabian Desert so fierce it left mountains of dust in the city, on everything, even in the air we breathe. My apartment—the floors, covered in a fine red powder. Very scary, the squall came across the city of Amman like a red hand from Allah. God is Red, after all. Vine Deloria Jr. would be proud.

Camel Trek, 1993, Southern Jordan

LEANNE HOWE

Does he have fleas? Is it nerves? Or does he really have fleas?

Ten minutes into a freaking heavy rain shower in the Naqab desert
in southern Jordan, numerous waterfalls begin to roar over the
sandstone mountaintops and into the aqueducts the Nabataeans
made before Cleopatra's reign in Egypt. After 2,000 years the
cisterns still hold water. It's the damnedest thing.

Does he have fleas? Is it nerves? Or does he really have fleas?

My camel refuses to say, but he stops, then heads toward the
cistern. He must be remembering a thousand treks, his ancestors,
the taste of rain. Now I understand his attack of nerves. A bath.

Joy Ride, Midnight of the Cooling Winds, Amman 2010

LEANNE HOWE

Above, the elongated Milky Way, stars like shingles deck the horizon, good weather, 87 degrees. Driving through the streets of Amman at midnight, winds cool my face, sunburned by the desert sky. I stop and traipse in and out of small shops, open until dawn. One on every block. A guy selling water and nuts. Another juices and colas. Still another has dates from Iraq and baklava, a Lebanese delicacy of honey, pistachios, the thinnest of filo dough. Small pharmacies dot the neighborhood hills, easy walking distances for *Sitt* and *Jiddo*. Shops are attached to the houses and remind me of the streets in West Ada, Oklahoma. As a kid, I would walk with Granny to the local shops searching for vegetables that she could not grow in her garden. What did we trade for, I don't recall now. But tonight I find Queen Noor Street, and King Talal Street, and Trader Vic's, the bar in the Regency Hotel. Trader Vic's doesn't sell vegetables at midnight. Not ever. What am I looking for?

Joy riding home, I see my grandparents standing under a lamppost on Al Wifaq Street. What are they doing out so late? Both, long dead, then suddenly alive on Harmony Street in Amman, and I know I don't understand the pull of *Bilaad ash Sham*, but my life here, yes. That it plays out in two places at once, that the climate marks me with small details of the weather five years ago. Yes.

Allison Adelle Hedge Coke

Arriving in Jordan my first thought was to call my friend Ibrahim Nasrallah (a great poet-writer, painter, photographer), who I had read with previously in festivals in South America. I was traveling with my oldest son, Travis (a writer, also invited to come), and was specifically interested in visiting other poets and sharing poetry for peace. A friend of ours, Trevino, had just arrived, as well, and Ibrahim and his generous wife and family plucked the three of us up from the hotel and planted us in a living room that could have easily passed for a gallery, the walls lined with so many gorgeous original works. Later, we traveled by commuter bus to other areas and met many lovely people along the way, including a nurse named Besma who gave me armloads of figs and asked me to always remember her and her name (smiling).

Most every day we awoke to morning call and took long walks and long lunches and dinners, and on occasion shared a bit of our own writing, at times being shuffled about, but mostly on our own, enjoying people we admired and places that still press concise imagery in memory. Sufi musicians played often nearby, wedding parties seemed to happen every night, the food was exemplary, and we were able to meet many people and see some great local sites. My love and concern for Palestinian people has been present since I was a young kid and my father detailed the West Bank siege, and deepened while I worked with Somiya, my friend in insurance coding (Raleigh, late seventies), and while studying at Estelle Harmon's (LA, mid-eighties), where I met many more people from the region and heard enough chilling detail I was forever moved. Coming to Jordan brought the land and presence of place into the realm of story, song, and poetry, and I hold a fondness and gratefulness for all of this, to this day, and hope to return again soon.

Was Morning Call

ALLISON ADELLE HEDGE COKE

for Ibrahim & LeAnne

It was morning call streaming some emic encoding, ceremonial invitation, invocation mood altering song, stilling wanderlust premise into meditative contemplation, into internalized presence, familiar. After the first dawn, we awaited every other, from hotel rooftops or friends' balconies, juxtaposed there against sky and sound in shared sense no matter the difference. There is none, in that place. If you are in. We came to it. My son and I scan the edges of courtyards, alleyways, between building spaces for cats looking something like we haven't seen in cats before. Something specifically natured Amman, or anywhere else cityscaped we happened to move toward. It was figs, olives generously let into our armholds by Basma smiling or any number of wonderful soulful women who were so happy to meet us, thrilled we attempted language, fond with memories of attending schools in North America, back not long ago. It was whistles for children, clicks for calls, weddings every night in the lobby and ballroom, music, music, music and song. It was Sufi chanting away angers and misunderstandings when other people from our countries grieved them with inconsiderate proselytizings, demands, or senseless banter. It was feeling funny when called a savage and responding that's what they try to tell us about you, too, shared laughter echoing back, o Indi Ahmed. Art stunning apartment walls around Ibrahim Nasrallah and more writers' union poets. Wine, Palestinian, opened just for us after being bottled for so many decades discussion ensued to recall the variables. It was hummus for pennies, oil so soft, the scent of it, fragrant, endearing. It was *qahweh* for free and *chayi* for almost nothing. Bits of fruit and desserts given as samples simply to celebrate someone attempting to order in *Alearabia* like me. It was cab rides through asthma for fifty cents when others were charged so ridiculously we all gathered round to laugh at the foolishness. Camels and Bedouin camped on the road just outside town. Bedouin, calling us Bedouin, too. King's crows, hooded, black, white, black, hang around King Abdullah's grave, longing for royal handouts, tourists tolls, guilt debts, manners of monarchy. It was morning call streaming some emic encoding, invocation, mood altering, stilling brought us home in some shared known never faltering despite the bullets streaming, in spite of ourselves. Stilling for a song, singing.

The Visit

ALLISON ADELLE HEDGE COKE

Sfifeh, qabbah, radah, irdan, mawris, benayiq, diyal, hiijer—

Here, hawthorn, cypress, tall palms, tree with lions, apple tree, false tree, true tree,

the tree of scorpions, bunches of grape—

Here, ducks, geese, swans, border of the hand, pool/harp, roses/ birds, lilies, wide open eye, crowns, muscles/dragon fly—

Here, snowflake borders, turning round, bald palms, necktie, snowflakes, snails, feathers, chick peas & raisins—

Here, road of Egypt, thirteen, frogs in a pond, heart/locket, single spear, pretty carnation, double spears, old man's teeth, stick, saw, bachelor's cushion, eastern one, pegtops, baker's wife, zigzag, little ears of corn, cock's comb, old man upside down—

Here, apples, chicken's feet, watermelons, pattern of the heart, cauliflower, key of Hebron, cock, kohl bottle, four eggs in a pan, ladder, pigeon, rainbow—

Here, foreign rainbow/arch, flower pot, the snake and the serpent, wide open eyes, cow's eye, garden rose/rose in a bud—

Here, Moon of Ramallah, Damask Rose, foreign moon—

Here, mill wheat, crab, Moon of Bethlehem, orange blossom—

Here, red, green, silver, indigo, yellow-green, purple, black yellow, red-brown, wine-red—

Here, night sky hovers over *hiijer, diyal, benayiqm mawris, irdan, radah, quabbah, sfifeh—*

Here, we walk to sleep through stitched dreams, the king's crows, white/black. Through threaded glisten like stars waiting, light devouring dense abyss bit by bit. We follow footsteps in awakening, carry memory immersing each place embroidered into emic repose, to know, to know, to know.

Craig Santos Perez

Since my wife and I had our first child eighteen months ago, much of how I see and experience the world is through the eyes of being a new parent. I have become acutely aware of how children are exploited and denied innocence in many places around the world, whether it be through war, poverty, labor, trafficking, etc. In terms of the Middle East, the conflict between Israel and Palestine resonates in the Pacific because of the similar history of settler colonialism and military occupation. This poem tries to capture some of these parallels through the experience of children and the symbolism of stones.

the convention on the rights of the child

CRAIG SANTOS PEREZ

my 18-month-old daughter plays
in the sand at waikiki beach, touches
the shells and small rocks.

during the first intifada,
soldiers were ordered to *break
the bones of those throwing*

rocks. when my daughter is older,
i will teach her how our
ancestors were born from

the rocks of humatak bay, guam,
seven thousand miles from
palestine. how do you say *child*

in arabic? when my daughter is
older, i will teach her how
our ancestors built their thatched

homes atop stone pillars. today,
soldiers killed a teenager
in the gaza strip for throwing rocks

near the border fence. if children
comprise half the population of gaza,
how many have been arrested

and tortured? how do you say *please
stop* in arabic? when my daughter
is older, i will teach her how

settlers burned our ancestors'
homes, stole our land, and built
their legacies atop pillars of

fire. how many bones
does a soldier have to break
before a child will confess

to anything? if they are convicted,
i say they are only guilty of
wanting houses to emerge

from ruins, olive trees to
bloom from ashes, and rocks
to transform into prayers.

today, settlers firebombed a home
in the west bank, killing an
18-month-old baby. how do you say

playground in arabic? when my daughter
is older, we will travel to our home
island and visit the stone pillars

that remain in the jungle. together,
we will touch our foundations
with our broken hands and pray.

Natalie Diaz

My experience of the Middle East came through my brother who served in the US military and spent two years in Afghanistan. The brother in this poem is not my real-life brother but an image of him after he returned home from the war there.

The Elephants

NATALIE DIAZ

Hast thou not seen how thy Lord dealt with the possessor of the elephant?
—al-Fil, sura 105, Qur'an

My brother still hears the tanks
    when he is angry—they rumble like a herd of hot green
        elephants over the plowed streets inside him, crash through

the white oleanders lining my parents' yard
    during family barbeques, great scarred ears flapping, commanding
        a dust storm that shakes blooms from the stalks like
            wrecked stars.

One thousand and one sleepless nights
    bulge their thick skulls, gross elephant boots pummel
        ice chests, the long barrels of their trunks crush cans of
            cheap beer

and soda pop in quick, sparking bursts of froth,
    and the meat on the grill goes to debris in the flames
        while the rest of us cower beneath lawn chairs.

When the tusked animals in my brother's miserable eyes
    finally fall asleep standing up, I find the nerve to ask him
        what they sound like, and he tells me, It's no hat dance,

and says that unless I've felt the bright beaks of ancient
Stymphalian birds,
    unless I've felt the color red raining from Heaven and marching
        in my veins, I'll never know the sound of war.

SPIRIT

But I do know that since my brother's been back,
    the orange clouds hang above him like fruit made of smoke,
        and he sways in a trancelike pachyderm rhythm

to the sweet tings of death music circling
    circling his head like an explosion of bluebottle flies
        haloing him—I'm no saint, he sighs, flicking each one away.

He doesn't sit in chairs anymore and is always on his feet,
    hovering by the window, peeking out the door, Because,
        he explains, everyone is the enemy, even you, even me.

The heat from guns he'll never let go
    rises up from his fists like a desert mirage, blurring
        everything he tries to touch or hold—

If we cry when his hands disappear like that, he laughs,
    these hands, he tells us, those little Frankensteins
        were never my friends.

But before all this, I waited for him
    as he floated down the airport escalator in his camouflage BDUs.
        An army-issued duffel bag dangles from his shoulders—

hot green elephants,
    their arsenal of memory, rocking inside.
        He was home. He was gone.

Prayer for Syria

DIANE GLANCY

> *. . . the shepherd takes out of the mouth of the lion*
> *two legs or a piece of an ear . . .*
> —Amos 3:12

1.
The mountains of the southern California desert
look far away and docile.
They would not erupt.
Yet the ground is settled with dark soil and rock—
volcanic in their beginning.
Syria, when I was there,
was barren as the California desert.
Eruption was a possibility, even then.
I see long trains in the distance like refugees streaming across the
borders of Turkey, Jordan, Lebanon, Afghanistan.

2.
In the mountains of Arizona there is rain.
East of Flagstaff, the odometer on my car
turns 200,000 miles. I wanted to see it when it did,
but was watching the rain that turned icy
in the higher altitude.

Two large trucks pass side by side in the west-bound lanes
throwing trails of water behind them.

3.
Now in the darkness, the one bright light of a
    train
coming from the east passes in the desert of New
    Mexico.

Brush off your suit, Bashar al-Assad—
adjust your neck-tie, polish your shoes.
You may be called to stand before the living God
with those bodies you've collected at your side.

Girls Targeted in Taliban Gas Attack

DIANE GLANCY

The pupils were lining up outside their classrooms for morning
assembly when one girl suddenly collapsed unconscious
—The Independent, London, May 13, 2009, Jerome Starkey

""She was only little," said Gulcheena, a 13-year-old student
Of the school who fell ill herself moments later."

"They were among 90 Afghan school girls
Unconscious and vomiting, possibly victims of a gas-
Poisoning attack on their school in Mahmud Raqi village."

"It was the third attack against a girls' school in
Afghanistan in as many weeks, raising the fears
That the Taliban are resorting to increasingly vicious methods
To terrorize young women out of education."

"Gulcheena described the gas as smelling like a chemical
Known locally as Mallatin, which farmers sometimes
Spread on fields to poison foraging birds."

II.
I would have driven there if I could
But the ocean is no place for driving.

Just a little poison
Sprayed into the courtyard of a school.

Why are they afraid if girls learn?
Would it also make them destroyers of songbirds
Who are girls that want to learn?
If meaning is in knowledge

Then it must be something undesirable—

But look at the marks of the letters they make
Curled back as the foot of a bird in flight.
Listen to the *click click* of the cricket
In the courtyard.
See how the sound of it can be written
Quiet as the ticking of a car bomb.

Linda Rodriguez

In discussions as contributions arrived, Diane Glancy, Ben Furnish, and I decided we wanted a poet's reflections on the wider context behind this anthology. The concept for this anthology was originally inspired by the firestorm that surrounded Joy Harjo's decision a few years ago to honor her commitment to visit Israel, hoping to spark a dialogue, in spite of the movement to boycott Israel for its appalling treatment of the population of Gaza. We wanted to gather a range of Native voices and experiences with no prior selection or restraint of what attitudes they should take to the tragic violence throughout the Middle East.

To our surprise, none of our contributors took an overtly political stance. To our delight, all of our contributors focused on the personal, the people, culture, and landscape, leading to the editorial decision that the book needed to give a brief contextual background for the poems.

In giving that historical and political context, I did not want to focus on Israel and Palestine. All too often in the United States, "the Middle East" simply means Israel and Palestine, ignoring the rich variety of cultures and countries that make up that part of the world and ignoring the history of overt and covert intervention by Western powers, especially Britain and the United States, that has led to the chaos that reigns over the entire region today. Very little is known about that history by most of the American public today.

By the time I wrote this essay, the vast majority of the contributions had arrived, and it seemed to me that they did have an underlying political implication—a celebration of the people and the land and a recognition of a fundamental correlation between the people they met and the contributors' own peoples. The book itself is a tribute to the enduring strength of Indigenous peoples everywhere and the sense that, as the poet Ahimsa Timoteo Bodhrán says, "Each of us is Indigenous somewhere."

Are Our Hands Clean?

A Meditation on the Middle East and the United States

BY LINDA RODRIGUEZ

The acapella singing group, Sweet Honey in the Rock, performs a song about the abuse and exploitation of poor women's labor around the world in order to bring Americans cheap clothing, and the song's refrain is a haunting, "Are my hands clean?" Thinking about the violence and chaos in the Middle East today with an estimated 400,000 deaths in Syria and over eight million desperate refugees leaves me with the same disturbing thought.

The United States has a long history in the Middle East, as it is constituted today—and of course, it is constituted artificially as it is today entirely because of what the Western powers wanted politically in that area of the world. US policy in the Middle East began in the 1940s, guided by our greed for oil and our support for Israel, and those two touchstones of our policy have remained our overriding goals in the region.

The United States' justification for all of our interventions in the Middle East, covert and overt, has always been and still is some version of the nineteenth century British "white man's burden," i.e., the citizens of the area are too uncivilized and benighted to rule themselves, so the United States must bring civilization, enlightenment, and democracy to those dark lands. Most people in the United States have long recognized what a mistake this was for the British, but the United States government blindly continues to make the same mistake that the British Empire did.

For Indigenous people in the United States, this is particularly problematic because we still remember how the British colonists and then the new Americans came to our nations with that same attitude of contempt for any culture other than their own and that same sense of entitlement to our lands and natural resources. We remember what it was like to be forced into different areas, often yoked with other peoples with whom we had little in common, and to have our own ways of structuring our societies destroyed by invaders who often installed corrupt puppet leaders and made legal agreements with people who had no right to give tribal land or make binding agreements for the Native nations.

We see these same events happening in the Middle East—and always it is the women, children, and elders who suffer the most. In Iraq, the killing that the US and its allies inflicted on the populace between 2003 and 2008 left 4.5 million children without one or both parents. Over one million women who are heads of households and the children living in those households live in poverty in a land where American extreme poverty is considered middle class. Millions live without access to reliable electric services or water, as the infrastructure has been destroyed. All of this has helped lead to the radicalization of young men who were children and teens during those awful years, and with the consequent rise of ISIL and other sectarian violence, the violent death rate is moving again to levels we have not seen since 2008.

Everything the United States government does and says is viewed with skepticism in the Middle East because of this country's deplorable history of meddling in the region's political affairs with ulterior motives. For example, Syria, which had become an independent republic in 1946, went through a coup d'état by the Army Chief of Staff, who was encouraged and aided in this by the CIA in exchange for favorable oil trade agreements. After that, the United States continued to support dictators in Syria for years. When Syria had once again formed a republican government, the US supported the transfer of power, instead, from the late Hafez al-Assad to his son, leading to the civil war that is devastating that country today.

Also, the United States and Israel played a role in that civil war,

believing that a weakened al-Assad was their best bet as a leader of Syria who could not pose a credible threat to their interests, so their covert agencies encouraged and supported the rebel movement against al-Assad, pulling their support when that began to become too successful, thus leading to what should have been the rebels' defeat. The rebels have continued fighting, however, embittered about the Western world. They are now having to fight both al-Assad's military and the ISIL forces, and the Western and then Russian bombing of Syria under these circumstances only pounds in that bitterness toward the developed world and helps it turn to hatred.

Of course, the United States has long had a policy of encouraging and then turning on allies in the Arab world. Our government encouraged the Kurds and Shias of Iraq to rise up against Saddam Hussein, promising support and ultimate victory, but in the actual fact of both revolts, the US did almost nothing for either group and allowed horrible reprisals from Hussein's forces to be taken against them.

Too often, our government supports dictators of the worst sort in the Middle East. We put the Shah of Iran in place, overthrowing a democratic regime that was about to nationalize Iran's oil fields, and in our quest for commercial control of the oil, we laid the foundations for the bloody reign of the ayatollahs. We helped both Saddam Hussein and Muammar Gaddafi to come to power and supported them until we felt it was no longer in our interests. We supported military coups in Tunisia and Algeria and the repressive governments of Egypt and Turkey. The two biggest problem actors that the United States government supports in the Middle East, however, are the governments of Saudi Arabia and Israel.

I won't go into great detail with Israel because the news media is frequently full of new atrocities they have directed toward the people of Gaza. I will remind you of only one thing: Israel, a country founded on humane principles, as was the United States, has become a country of apartheid for Palestinians, whose land it originally was.

Saudi Arabia's actions receive less scrutiny from the media than even Israel's do. Yet Saudi Arabia violates the human rights of the majority of people who live within its borders, violently suppresses all dissent and opposition, invaded Bahrain with tanks to destroy its budding democratic movement, and is currently bombing Yemen, killing and injuring thousands of innocent civilians—and Saudia Arabia uses American missiles, fighters, bombers, tanks, weapons, and military training to do all of these things with our implicit approval.

At the same time, Saudi Arabia has exported one of the most extremist forms of Islam all across the world. It is no coincidence that fifteen of the nineteen terrorists who carried out the 9/11 attacks in the United States were Saudis, as was Osama bin Laden, who continued to draw financial support from Saudi Arabia until his death. In the US, we are horrified at the cruel beheadings ISIL has committed, but Saudi Arabia beheaded 158 people in 2015, according to Amnesty International, many for nonviolent crimes, such as drug possession, adultery, and apostasy.

Between them, the governments of Israel and Saudi Arabia have caused a great amount of unrest in the Middle East, all with massive American financial and military support, but we as a country still continue to be a major force for chaos and violence in the region, as we try to maintain our political and military hegemony over the oil-rich territory.

Our leaders, for too long, have ignored the real people who live in these countries and suffer from our policies and actions, just as they have ignored the real Americans in our military who also suffer from our policies and actions. In both cases, the American government has shown itself unwilling to deal with the damage it has done and has left the American soldiers and the

Middle Eastern citizens to struggle with the attempt to rebuild lives, homes, and countries.

All of this is difficult for many Indigenous people in the United States. As citizens and taxpayers, these wrongs have been committed in our name. As the descendants of survivors of genocide and ethnic cleansing, a number of us find the violence and chaos the US and its allies have visited on the Middle East repugnant, and when we look at the problems of violence, poverty, and dysfunction that plague many of our own communities as the trauma of Manifest Destiny has worked its way through the generations, we realize what a terrible and difficult task of personal and community survival lies ahead for the people of the Middle East—if all the bombing and violence could stop now. Since there appears no evidence of any cessation or even slowing of the escalation of violence in the region, that task only becomes more daunting every day.

As a person of Indigenous heritage and an American citizen and taxpayer, I weep at what is being done in my name and with my money. For years, I have signed petitions, protested, and voted against these mad and cruel policies that do not benefit American citizens but rather the billionaire owners and investors in huge corporations. I know many other Indigenous (and non-Indigenous) people who have done the same. Yet it is all for naught. The power structure continues to wield its power and do what will bring it more money and power without any thought for the future consequences. The bombing and the undermining of regimes and the blank checks to Israel and Saudi Arabia continue.

No hands are clean in this country.

What can we then do under such hopeless-seeming circumstances? Following in the footsteps of our ancestors, we can refuse to give up the fight. We can continue to protest, to vote, to politically organize, and to write, using our voices to remind the United States and the world that there are real human beings under those bombs, real families with vulnerable children and fragile elders at the other end of this country's support for oppressive regimes and violence in the region to increase the profits of a few corporations. This book, in many ways, attempts to show that humanity as witnessed through the perspectives of different individuals.

And if it becomes clear that nothing we can do will change these destructive policies, if, like our ancestors, we face certain defeat, we can do what our ancestors did as they attacked against overwhelming odds or faced execution or walked the Trail of Tears—we can sing.

Song has always been central to Indigenous culture and is one aspect that is found in all of the more than five hundred nations. We sing to pray because we believe the world was created to be harmonious and balanced, and we seek to bring it back into that harmony and balance. We sing to communicate with our Creator. We sing to heal and to celebrate. We sing to give honor to those who have traveled on before us. We sing to ask for their help in our own journey and to ask those whom we leave behind to remember us and what we tried to do.

This book is our song.

BIOGRAPHIES

Jim Barnes

Jim Barnes is the author or editor of several books of poetry, prose, translation, and criticism. He taught at Truman State University from 1970 to 2003 and later became the Distinguished Professor of English and Creative Writing at Brigham Young University until 2006. In 2009, he was named Oklahoma Poet Laureate.

He was the founding editor of Chariton Review Press, the editor of *The Chariton Review*, and contributing editor for the Pushcart Prize.

He has received a National Endowment for the Arts Fellowship, the Columbia University Translation Award, the St. Louis Poetry Center's Stanley Hanks Memorial Poetry Award, and the Rockefeller Foundation's Bellagio Residency Fellowship.

Barnes is of Choctaw decent.

Kimberly Blaeser

Kimberly Blaeser (Anishinaabe) is a widely published creative writer, photographer, and scholar. A professor at University of Wisconsin-Milwaukee, she teaches Native American literatures and creative writing.

Blaeser has authored three collections of poetry, most recently *Apprenticed to Justice*, and is the Wisconsin Poet Laureate for 2015–16. She is also the author of the scholarly monograph *Gerald Vizenor: Writing in the Oral Tradition*, and among her edited volumes is *Traces in Blood, Bone, and Stone: Contemporary Ojibwe Poetry*.

Blaeser has performed her work at over three hundred different venues around the globe, from Bahrain to Spain, and identifies the two most memorable sites for readings as the Borobudur Temple in Indonesia and a Fire-Ceremony at the Borderlands Museum Grounds in arctic Norway. Selections of her poetry have been translated into several languages including Spanish, Norwegian, Indonesian, Hungarian, and French.

She has been the recipient of awards for both writing and speaking, among these a Wisconsin Arts Board Fellowship in Poetry and four Pushcart nominations. An editorial board member for the "American Indian Lives" series of the University of Nebraska

Press and for the "Native American Series" of Michigan State University Press, Blaeser has also served on the advisory board for the Sequoyah National Research Center and Native American Press Archives and on the Poetry Fellowship Panel for the National Endowment for the Arts.

Her current work, which brings her poetry and photography together in new form she calls "picto-poems," has been featured in two exhibits and is forthcoming in an art chapbook.

Trevino L. Brings Plenty

Trevino L. Brings Plenty is a poet and musician who lives, works, and writes in Portland, Oregon. He is a singer/songwriter/guitarist for the musical ensemble Ballads of Larry Drake. He has read/ performed his work at poetry festivals as far away as Amman, Jordan and close to his home base at Portland's Wordstock Festival.

In college, Trevino worked with Primus St. John and Henry Carlile for this poetry work, studied with Tomás Svoboda for music composition, and Jerry Hahn for jazz guitar.

Trevino is an American and Native American; a Lakota Indian born on the Cheyenne River Sioux Reservation, South Dakota, USA. Some of his work explores the American Indian identity in American culture and how it has through, genealogical history, affected indigenous peoples in the twenty-first century. He writes of urban Indian life; it's his subject.

Other titles by the author: *Wakpá Wanáǧi, Ghost River*; *Real Indian Junk Jewelry*; *Shedding Skins: Four Sioux Poets*.

Natalie Diaz

Natalie Diaz was born and raised in the Fort Mojave Indian Village in Needles, California. She is Mojave and an enrolled member of the Gila River Indian Tribe.

Her first poetry collection, *When My Brother Was an Aztec*, was published by Copper Canyon Press in April of 2012. Her poems received the *Narrative* Prize and appeared in *Best American Poetry* and the annual *Pushcart Prize* collection.

She is the recipient of a Lannan Residency in Marfa, Texas;

a Native Arts & Culture Foundation Arts Fellowship; a Lannan Literary Fellowship, a Holmes National Poetry Prize, a Bread Loaf Scholarship and Fellowship, and a United States Artist Fellowship.

DIANE GLANCY

Diane Glancy is professor emerita at Macalester College. She is mixed-blood, undocumented Cherokee. Her 2014-15 books are *Fort Marion Prisoners and the Trauma of Native Education*, nonfiction, University of Nebraska Press, and *Report to the Department of the Interior*, poetry, University of New Mexico Press, which won the 2016 Willa Award from Women Writers of the West.

She also published three novels, *Uprising of Goats*, *One of Us*, and *Ironic Witness*, Wipf & Stock. A new collection of poems, *The Collector of Bodies: Concern for Syria and the Middle East*, was published by Wipf & Stock in 2016.

Among her awards are a 2014 Native Writers Circle of the Americas Lifetime Achievement Award, an American Book Award, and two National Endowment for the Arts Fellowships. In 2016, she won the Lubbe Manuscript Award from the Poetry Society of Texas. *WERTYUIOPASDFGHJKLZXCVBNM, The Keyboard Letters*, will be published in 2017. Native Voices at the Autry in Los Angeles has produced four of her plays.

Her other books and information are listed on her websites: www.dianeglancy.com, www.dianeglancy.org. Glancy lives in Kansas and Texas.

JOY HARJO

Joy Harjo of the Mvskoke Nation is an acclaimed poet, musician, writer and performer. She has released four albums of original music and won a NAMMY for best female artist. Her one-woman show, *Wings of Night Sky, Wings of Morning Light*, premiered in Los Angeles and will soon be a book. She has a commission from The Public Theater of NYC to write the musical play *We Were There When Jazz Was Invented*, which will revise the origin story of American music to include Southeastern indigenous music.

She was featured on HBO's *Def Poetry Jam, PBS NewsHour*

with *Jim Lehrer*, and a Bill Moyers series on poetry. She travels internationally to perform solo and with her band the Joy Harjo.

Her seven books of award-winning poetry include *She Had Some Horses* and her newest, *Conflict Resolution for Holy Beings*.

Her awards include the New Mexico Governor's Award for Excellence in the Arts, a Rasmussen US Artists Fellowship, the William Carlos Williams Award from the Poetry Society of America, and a Guggenheim Fellowship. She is at work on a new album of original music. She lives in the Mvskoke Nation in Oklahoma.

ALLISON ADELLE HEDGE COKE

Allison Hedge Coke was born in the Texas Panhandle and grew up in North Carolina, Canada, and on the Great Plains, where she currently lives in Oklahoma. She came of age sharecropping tobacco and worked in factories, fields, and waters. She has Cherokee, Huron, Métis, French Canadian, Portuguese, Scottish, English, and Irish heritage.

She is on the faculty of the Red Earth MFA program at Oklahoma City University and Vermont College of Fine Arts MFA in Writing & Publishing. Her books include *Streaming, Blood Run, Off-Season City Pipe, Dog Road Woman, Sing, Effigies, Effigies II,* and *Rock, Ghost, Willow, Deer: a Story of Survival*.

Among honors she has received an American Book Award, the King-Chavez-Parks Award, the 2015 Wordcrafter of the Year Award, the 2015 Native Writers' Circle of the Americas Lifetime Achievement Award, the 2015 PEN Southwest Book Award, and the 2016 Library of Congress Witter Bynner Fellowship.

TRAVIS HEDGE COKE

Born in North Carolina, Travis Hedge Coke is a professor at Shandong University and a writes regularly for The Comics Cube (www.comicscube.com).

His work can be found in *The Willow's Whisper: A Transatlantic Compilation of Poetry from Ireland and Native America*, recordings for *The Lumberyard,* and in literary journals including *Hawai'i Review, riverbabble,* and *The Florida Review*. He is a founding editor of *Future Earth Magazine*, a former editor of *Platte Valley Review*, and associate editor of *Sing: Poetry from the Indigenous Americas*. He lives in Weihai, a city not unlike those in North Carolina, situated between the seaside and mountains.

LINDA HOGAN

A Chickasaw novelist, essayist, and environmentalist, Linda Hogan was born in Denver, Colorado. She earned an undergraduate degree from the University of Colorado Colorado Springs and an MA in English and creative writing from the University of Colorado Boulder.

Hogan is the author of the poetry collections *Calling Myself Home*; *Daughters, I Love You*; *Eclipse*; *Seeing Through the Sun*, which won the American Book Award from the Before Columbus Foundation; *Savings*; *The Book of Medicine*s, a National Book Critics Circle Award finalist; and *Rounding the Human Corners*. Intimately connected to her political and spiritual concerns, Hogan's writing deals with environmental issues, the perspective of Native Americans, or historical narratives, including oral histories. William Kittredge, in his introduction to Hogan's *Rounding the Human Corners*, noted, "poets like Linda, through their language, open for us a doorway into their specific resonating dream of the electric universe."

A recipient of grants from the National Endowment for the Arts and the Guggenheim Foundation for her fiction, Hogan's novels include *Mean Spirit*, a Pulitzer finalist, *Solar Storms*, *Power*, and *People of the Whale: A Novel*.

Active as a speaker, Hogan taught at the University of Colorado and at the Indigenous Education Institute. She has been a speaker at the United Nations Forum and was a plenary speaker at the Environmental Literature Conference in Turkey in 2009.

Hogan's awards include a Lannan Literary Award, the Mountains and Plains Booksellers Spirit of the West Literary Achievement Award, and a Lifetime Achievement Award from the Native Writers' Circle of the Americas.

LeAnne Howe

LeAnne Howe is the author of novels, plays, poetry, screenplays, and scholarship that deal with Native experiences. A Choctaw Nation of Oklahoma citizen, her latest book, *Choctalking on Other Realities* won the inaugural 2014 MLA Prize for Studies in Native American Literatures, Cultures, and Languages.

She received the Western Literature Association's 2015 Distinguished Achievement Award. Other awards include the Fulbright Scholarship 2010–2011; the 2012 Lifetime Achievement Award from the Native Writers' Circle of the Americas; and a 2012 United States Artists Ford Fellowship.

She is the Eidson Distinguished Professor of American Literature in English at the University of Georgia. Howe's current projects include a new book, *Savage Conversations*, set for 2017, and a novel set in the Middle East.

Bojan Louis

Bojan Louis is a member of the Navajo Nation—Naakai Dine'é; Ashiihí; Ta'neezahnii; Bilgáana.

His poems have appeared or are forthcoming in *The Kenyon Review*, *Platte Valley Review*, *Hinchas de Poesía*, *American Indian Culture and Research Journal*, and *Black Renaissance Noire*; his fiction in *Alaska Quarterly Review*, *Yellow Medicine Review*, and *Off the Path Volume II: An Anthology of 21st Century American Indian and Indigenous Writers*; his creative nonfiction in *As/Us Journal* and *MudCity Journal*. He is the author of the nonfiction chapbook, *Troubleshooting Silence in Arizona*. His poetry book *Currents* is forthcoming from BkMk Press.

He has been a resident at The MacDowell Colony. Recently a full-time English Instructor at Arizona State University's Downtown Campus, he is currently teaching in Spain. Formerly co-editor at *Waxwing,* he is currently poetry editor at *RED INK: An International Journal of Indigenous Literature, Art, & Humanities*.

CRAIG SANTOS PEREZ

Craig Santos Perez is a native Chamoru (Chamorro) from the Pacific Island of Guåhan (Guam).

He is the co-founder of Ala Press, co-star of the poetry album *Undercurrent*, and author of three collections of poetry, most recently *from unincorporated territory [guma']*, which received the American Book Award.

His writing explores themes of indigenous identity, militarism, decolonization, food sovereignty, ecological imperialism, migration, and citizenship.

He is an Associate Professor in the English Department, and affiliate faculty with the Center for Pacific Islands Studies and the Indigenous Politics Program at the University of Hawai'i at Mānoa, where he teaches Pacific literature and creative writing.

LINDA RODRIGUEZ

Linda Rodriguez's three novels featuring Cherokee campus police chief, Skeet Bannion—*Every Hidden Fear*, *Every Broken Trust*, and *Every Last Secret*—have received critical recognition and awards, such as Latina Book Club Best Book of 2014, St. Martin's Press/Malice Domestic Best First Traditional Mystery Novel Award, selections of Las Comadres National Latino Book Club, 2nd Place in the International Latino Book Awards, finalist for the Premio Aztlán Literary Prize, 2014 ArtsKC Fund Inspiration Award, and Barnes & Noble mystery pick. Her short story, "The Good Neighbor," published in the anthology, *Kansas City Noir*, has been optioned for film.

For her books of poetry, *Skin Hunger* and *Heart's Migration*, Rodriguez received numerous awards and fellowships, including the Thorpe Menn Award for Literary Excellence, the Midwest Voices and Visions Award, the Elvira Cordero Cisneros Award, the 2011 ArtsKC Fund Inspiration Award, and Ragdale and Macondo fellowships.

Rodriguez was 2015 chair of the AWP Indigenous-Aboriginal American Writers Caucus, immediate past president of the Border Crimes chapter of Sisters in Crime, a founding board member of

Latino Writers Collective and The Writers Place, and a member of International Thriller Writers, Wordcraft Circle of Native American Writers and Storytellers, and Kansas City Cherokee Community. She is also the author of *Plotting the Character-Driven Novel* (2016) Find her at http://lindarodriguezwrites.blogspot.com.

KIM SHUCK

Kim Shuck's poetry collection *Smuggling Cherokee* won the Diane Decorah award in 2005. Other publications include the poetry collection *Clouds Running In,* the poetry anthology *Oakland Out Loud: Poetry and Prose in Celebration of "There,"* co-edited with Karla Brundage, and the chapbook *Sidewalk Ndn.* She lives in San Francisco, California.

JAMES THOMAS STEVENS

James Thomas Stevens, Aronhió:ta's, was born in Niagara Falls, New York in 1966. He attended the Institute of American Indian Arts and The Jack Kerouac School of Disembodied Poetics at Naropa, and received his MFA from Brown University.

Stevens, recipient of a 2000 Whiting Award, is the author of *A Bridge Dead in the Water, Combing the Snakes from His Hair, Bulle/Chimère, Mohawk/Samoa:Transmigrations* with Caroline Sinavaiana, *Of Kingdoms and Kangaroo* with Nicolas Destino and *(dis)Orient.* He is a member of the Akwesasne Mohawk Nation and teaches Creative Writing at the Institute of American Indian Arts. Stevens lives in Cañoncito, New Mexico.

Acknowledgments

Jim Barnes: Another version of "Goshen Tavern" appeared in *The Fish on Poteau Mountain* (Cedar Creek Press).

Kimberly Blaeser: "Voices in the Desert, Bahrain 2010," "Unlawful Assembly," *New Letters*.

Natalie Diaz: "The Elephants" from *When My Brother Was an Aztec*. Copyright © 2012 by Natalie Diaz. Reprinted with the permission of The Permissions Company, Inc., on behalf of Copper Canyon Press, www.coppercanyonpress.org.

Diane Glancy: "The Whole of What Story," *Front Porch Journal*; "Bedouin Girl Reads About Transportation in Russia," *Image: A Journal of the Arts and Religion*; "Girls Targeted in Taliban Gas Attack," "Prayer for Syria," *New Letters*; "Down to the Simplest Wire in the Human Voice," "Private Dinner, March 28," *Quarter After Eight*; "Necessary Departures," *The Final Crusade: A Global Anthology*.

Joy Harjo: "Refugee," *New Letters*.

LeAnne Howe: "Camel Trek, 1993, Southern Jordan," "Joy Ride, Midnight of the Cooling Winds, Amman, 2010," *New Letters*.

Bojan Louis: "To Sugar a Dream," *New Letters*.

Kim Shuck: "In the Southern Desert," "Water to Water," *New Letters*.